T0065445

Manifestation Mantras
for
Soul Healing, Self Mastery &
Creating a Better Life

A Book of Divinely Channeled Mantras
to Assist with Your Mind, Body,
Energy & Soul Healing Journey to
CHANGE YOUR LIFE!

Jessica Hope Williams

BALBOA.PRESS
A DIVISION OF HAY HOUSE

Balboa Press books may be ordered through booksellers or by contacting:

Balboa Press
A Division of Hay House
1663 Liberty Drive
Bloomington, IN 47403
www.balboapress.com
844-682-1282

Print information available on the last page.

ISBN: 978-1-9822-5989-1 (sc)
ISBN: 978-1-9822-5990-7 (e)

Balboa Press rev. date: 12/21/2020

Manifestation Mantras
For
Soul Healing, Self
Mastery &
Creating a Better Life

Jessica Hope Williams, T.T, QHHT, RMT

Table of Contents:

Manifestation Mantras
for
Soul Healing, Self
Mastery & Creating a
Better Life

I	II	III	IV	V	VI	VII
Opening Credits:	Introduction	The Mantras	Bonus Notes & Quotes	Conclusion	About the Author	Message to The Reader

Introduction:

Jessica's book, "Manifestation Mantras for Soul Healing, Self Mastery & Creating a Better Life" is for everyone and anyone on any level of their spiritual journey; even for those of you just curious to see what using true manifestation techniques and mantras can truly create in your life.

Remember, with any practice it must be done consistently and with purpose and focus on intention. Anything done in a negative mindset or belief system will of course create results that aren't particularly favorable to the person adopting the practice.

When using these Mantras, please keep in mind your intention and being mindful of keeping your energy focused on what it is that you DO want to create and keep your focus OFF of what you DO NOT want to manifest for yourself.

It is vital and imperative that you as the one whom is seeking to create for yourself a new and better experiences in your reality; are practicing these mantras consciously and responsibly.

What does this mean? If you feel that you are not aligned with your own soul or soul purpose, or perhaps you feel you have strayed away from your true inner self and happiness / inner peace – It is important than through your journey with these Mantras, for you to consciously work on creating and allowing this alignment to happen gradually as well.

This is a part of being spiritually mature and being responsible for our own spirit and our own journey. You may practice these Mantras as many times a day as you feel is necessary & fully encourage you to use your intuition to find your won practice and flow with them as well.

Welcome: Your New Manifestation
Mastery Practice is Inside…….

~BREATHE~

May your soul healing journey
deepen with every divinely
channeled mantra & command in this book

~

May you learn the power of these
ancient practices long forgotten
and now being remembered once more

~

May you boldly take back the
power over your life with these
powerful words and miraculously
manifest a more whole and
beautiful reality for yourself
& into your LIFE!

The Manifestation Mantras

In the Infinite
flow of the
mystery of life…

I deeply appreciate
& feel gratitude
for the beauty that
is within & all
around me

大光明

Self Mastery

Today I consciously
Choose to open my mind,
my heart, my spirit &
my life to a healthier,
more positive way of
living.

I AM taking the steps to
make this happen for myself now!

Breathe – Feel yourself
consciously creating this all
now.

Today I recognize that the only real thing stopping me from my success is ME.

I AM fully and consciously choosing in this & every moment to get out of my own way of my own personal success.

Now.

In this moment, I AM allowing the Divine Flow of pure light, pure divine bliss and joyfulness to fill my heart, mind, body & soul now.

I AM truly grateful for this gift from the Universe and the Creator today and every day.

Today, I consciously
choose to open my mind,
my heart, my spirit &
my life to a healthier,
more positive way of
living.

I AM taking the steps
to make things happen
now!

Breathe - Feel yourself
consciously creating
this now.

As I expand my
consciousness and my
awareness into the
blessings that life holds for
me...

I Breathe them all into
Creation NOW!

I hold the key to my life.
I write my story.

Live Golden

*There is Magic and
Mystery in letting go of
what you believed should
happen, and allowing
and opening up to Life
as it is unfolding its
Miracles for me today
and every day....*

Every day I give
gratitude to the Universe
for the breath of life and
the gift of another day
on Earth.

Every single moment of
Every single day is a
Gift.

Today I recognize that life is not always comfortable. At times it is quite painful. Even in the pain I surrender myself into the gift that is life, for without the stormy days we would not appreciate the blissful warmth of the Sun Rays.

~ This is the Balance ~

Today I connect my heart to the Love of the Universe.

As I open my heart, I expand my love into every aspect of my life.

As I do this I AM blessing all areas of my reality and my life with Divine Love.

As I allow myself to Ascend
into a lighter state of being

-

I free myself from all that
has kept me stagnant,
blocked and held me back from
creating the most beautiful
and powerful version
of myself & all that has held
me down.
I speak this into existence
NOW.

Today I proclaim that all self-limiting fears are no longer allowed to exist within me, nor in my life anymore.

I AM re-claiming my confidence and bravery over all of my steps in life moving forward.

It is time.

There is no elevation
without knowing what it
feels like to fall.
When we fall we
understand what it feels
like to pull ourselves back
up from the ground.

The only people who find
success are the people who
face the fear of failing
until they find it.

Today I AM
re-claiming my life back.

For all of the things I
believe that I cannot
accomplish; I AM
transforming those
beliefs into the knowing
that I can and I AM!
My future is Mine.
I hold the pen.

In this moment, I fully allow myself to outgrow all of the false ideals and false narratives that anyone including myself holds in their minds about me;

I AM now FREEING ME to authentically BE ME!

If Not Now.....

When?

-Italian Author: Primo Levi

Today I claim my success!

The only way to truly be successful is to wake up and decide: " I am going to take every step necessary, even when it pushes me far beyond my comfort zones, I choose to push forward towards my dreams and goals unapologetically."

Keep Life Simple:

Step 1. Make a Plan

Step 2. Bring the Plan to Life

Step 3. DO NOT give up on your plan.

Self Mastery

*Today I fully choose to
claim my unique purpose
in life.
I understand that many
people have many hats to
wear and many roles to
fill.
Today I fully embrace my
own unique purpose of my
soul and allow my soul to
fully unfold the beauty of
all that I AM unto this
life.*

Transform

In this moment I AM
fully embracing and
honoring my souls
purpose & my path.

I AM accepting completely
that even if sometimes I
do not feel it ~ I AM
beautiful.
I AM incredible.
I AM authentically
amazing.
I AM Loved.

Let the music of life
flow through you

~

Let it become one
with you.

The Universe is a
Symphony

*Today and Every Day
I AM taking back my
power and my
willingness to do the
work that it takes to
make my dream life
become my reality.*

Today and every day I
align my heart, mind, body
& soul with my mission
here on earth.
Nothing and No One can
stop me from achieving my
goals and my missions in
life.
I AM completely and
perfectly on my path.

Always.

Ascend

Today I AM deciding
that I know what I want
for myself & for my life.
I AM pushing myself
past my comfort zones &
taking all of the
necessary steps to make
these things happen
for me NOW.

Today I AM removing all doubt from my being.

I quiet my mind & listen to my heart.

The heart is the seat of the soul ~ Therefore I know my heart will not steer me wrong.

If I ever feel as if I
have lost my way

~

I remind myself that
I AM already perfectly
on my path right now.

Even when I feel lost,
it is a part of my
journey….

Today and in every
Moment
I and only I define within
myself what my purpose is
& what I choose for my
life.
What I cannot know and
what is left to the stars is
out of my control.
I choose to have full
acceptance of the divine
path as well.

In this moment....
I AM
allowing love from
others and also
from myself to
fully and
completely enter
into me NOW.

As worry and fear enter
my mind and my energy
field; I allow myself to
experience it respectfully &
then I consciously
bring my thoughts,
my emotions & my spirit
fully back into a perfect
sate of Divinity and
ultimate peace and inner
calmness.

In the face of opposition &
ignorance – Sometimes the
best response is silence.

~

Today I fully allow myself
the freedom from arguing
with ignorance.

I Forgive Them.

I AM FREE.

Love

Today I walk in Divine
Love.

~

I see with eyes of Love.

~

I act with Love at the
forefront of my heart, mind
body & soul.

Fear has NO power of me anymore.

Today & Every day I release ALL fears into the light NOW ~

I AM Happy
I AM Healthy
I AM Balanced
I AM Healed
I AM Whole
I AM Well

I AM in the best most
healthiest most perfectly
aligned state of being
wonderfully and beautifully
NOW!

I give myself fully
permission to believe and
know that I AM
beautiful inside & out.

~

I allow myself fully to see
myself as beautiful
inside and out from now
on. . . .

I Know ~ I AM.

Today I decide to honor my bravery to live in this vessel ~ This human form that I call my body, my heart, my mind & my spirit.

~

It is Brave to live as a human being and take on fully this life.

I AM Present. I AM Brave.

Change

On this day, in this moment

~

I fully choose to awaken the
strength that lives within
me.
I can choose to access this
strength at any moment
that I need to.

I AM thankful.

I AM STRONG.

As I learn to connect to the
Divine Intelligence of life
and Universal consciousness
itself & to the God Source of
Love and Divine Light;
I come to understand that I
AM naturally a part of this
intelligence & therefore I
an access this within me at
all times.
For this I AM infinitely
Grateful.

Even when I have doubts ~
I know inherently that I
AM deeply and purely loved
by the Universe & by those
that cherish me the most.
It is imperative that I love
myself, and so this love
begins within myself.
I AM un-conditionally
loved & for this I AM
grateful beyond measure.

I AM Confident

I AM Capable

I AM Skilled

I AM Important

I AM Talented

I AM Valuable to this World

I cannot master life by
changing the natural flow
to life itself.
To master life I must
accept the flow & natural
order of things ~ Through
this acceptance I can guide
my life through the ebbs
and flows by navigating my
own sails.
I AM going into the flow of
life fully NOW ~

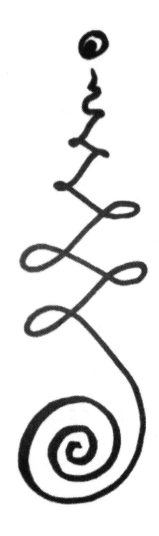

Today I allow myself to find
my center and balance
between my light & my
darkness completely both in
their purest form.
I AM in perfect harmony and
balance of my yin & my
yang energy as well as all
aspect of myself.

I create this for myself
perfectly NOW!

Bonus Notes and Quotes:

Light is repelled by darkness; but darkness is drawn to the light ~ darkness does not understand that it is simply the absence of light. One is not complete nor in balance without the other. Both believe they are superior to the other. This is the paradox of life."
- Jessica Hope Williams

"A familys' black sheep are actually liberators of their family tree. Family members who don't adapt to family rules or traditions, those who constantly try to revolutionize beliefs. Those who choose roads contrary to the well beaten paths of family lines; those who are criticized, judged and even rejected. These souls are often called to free the family from repetitive patterns that frustrate entire generations. These so-called "black sheep" - The ones that don't fit in, the ones that howl with rebellion, actually repair, detox and create new thriving branches in their family tree. Countless unrealistic desires, broken dreams or frustrated talents of our ancestors manifest themselves through this revolt. For inertia, the family tree will do anything to maintain the neutral and toxic course of its trunk, which will make the rebels task difficult and conflicting. Stop doubting and take care of your rarity. Like the most precious flower in your tree you are the dream of your ancestors."

~ Bert Hellinger

Love is the most powerful force in the world.
If people tell you that the opposite of love is fear,
it is not so. Love just is. Love has no opposite.
Remember that, dear one. Love has no opposite.
Love just is. It is the answer to
everything. Everything."
~ Dolores Cannon, The Convoluted Universe –
Book Two

**Go with Love in all things and
you'll always be prepared;
Always find balance ~ Balance in all things.**
~ Joseph Kerrigan

*In life, people plant a tree in the ground. This tree is
something physical, a representation of something
they hope to reap the rewards of later on. Rewards
of their hard work & diligence of watering the tree
and feeding it & watching it grow & thrive from
this consistent attention and love the tree is given.
Many that grow their tree or plants tend to watch
them regularly for signs of distress or needing more
water, sunlight, nourishment etc…
They observe the tree; is the tree happy? They*

wonder how much the tree will provide for them
when its reached its full capacity for bearing fruits.
Essentially the basic nature of a human being
"what can the tree do for me?"
Right? A tree is a tangible, physical living thing that we
can watch daily and wait patiently for it to give to
us what we want from it yes?
What about though when it comes to people?
Relationships? Our children? Our families?
Our partners & lovers?
All too often we tend to forget that when we
give unconditional love, sunlight, nourishment &
happiness to our loved ones, (and also to ourselves)
we strengthen
& nourish not only their bodies & minds but also
their spirits.
We see them come alive and their eyes brighten.
Ultimately through this consistent love and effort
& attentiveness we nourish them back into a state of
bliss and contentment and happiness and therefore
they provide to us in return the most vibrant
beautiful loving versions of themselves;
just as they were when we first fell in love with who
they are. This is in my opinion a beautiful exchange
of energy given.

I invite you to ask yourself; In such a fast paced day and age for humanity... Aren't our loved one's worth it to us to love & to nourish them regularly, just as we would for something such as a tree that we mostly only take care of to get something in return from it?

It's quite a self-centered way to view love that humanity has adopted when we really sit with it....
Isn't it?
Let's be better humans shall we? May we Love each other back to life when life feels too hard to do it for ourselves.... May we patiently nourish our loved ones and ourselves when we need it most ~ so that we may reap the rewards of experiencing the best most beautiful version of ourselves.

~ Jessica H. Williams

Bonus Notes and Quotes:

Sometimes the only true peace between you & someone you want to make peace with is the peace you create within yourself; and that's okay.
~ Jessica H. Williams

We are all connected by an invisible web ~ it brings us together and binds us to one another & through that web we grow & change the very universe itself.
~ Edwin A. Pacheco

The art of taking care of yourself is a painting ~ a vast one at that. It never ends…. Taking care of yourself does not stop after you've painted yourself; understand one's self is just the key piece of carin. Then it extends to others, your family, anyone that cares for you in any way. Once you understand the balance of yourself and he people around you, the painting is complete ~ more importantly you've learned true self-worth.
~ Gabriel Zion Williams

"You are the fiery life of divine substance, you blaze above the beauty of the fields, you shine in the waters, you burn in the sun, moon and stars."
~ Hildegard Von Bingen

Conclusion:

In conclusion, the main point of this book is simple yet powerful. Throughout history of mankind, there is ample record of people using their words through song, spells, even sorcerers and wizards speaking what they desire to create powerfully into their reality.

Most of us have grown up being indoctrinated with this story that none of us are powerful and all of the power belongs to those outside of us who we deem as more powerful; first God / Universe / Creator (Whatever the word you use for the Source of all Creation.)

Secondly some of us have learned to call on Angels or Dietes etc... Some people use magical spells, rituals, etc.. The list goes on.

The point is, even during the time that the
Christian bible was written after the one we call
Jesus in the Christian Religion, is the quote
where Jesus was doing Divine Healings
and Energy Healing work and the people of the
village said that he was performing miracles.
To this Jesus was said to reply, "This is nothing,
you will learn to do this and so much more."

In the beginning of my Energy Healing
practice when I started studying my gift I
came to learn that phrase above from Jesus from my first
Master Teacher and it stuck with me because
I grew up going to a Christian church and
always knew I could work with energy but
never understood why some of the things that
Jesus was said to be able to do, seemed
normal to me.
There is much I could share here but I would
like to keep things simple in this book and easy to grasp
and therefore I will I leave you off with this.….

Whether you are just beginning your spiritual
journey or you are a Master Healer / Teacher etc...
My point in creating this book of Mantras is to
share with you and the world the powerful
commands and mantras that I have intuited
through my own channeling gifts that have
helped so many of my clients, and of
course myself; and will hopefully
help so many more along the way.
I feel that at this point in
humanities evolution that we are at an apex of change.

This moment is pivotal; We must take
responsibility for our own lives and our own
abilities to create and manifest what we want and
what happens in our lives. With so much
information at everyone's finger tips these days
and spiritual teachings and energy being such a
big topic now – It is only right for the proper
information and teachings to find their way into
the hands of all whom are ready to evolve into the
powerful beings that you already are inside.

These Mantras are a stepping stone into assisting you in creating a new way of thinking and speaking what you desire into your life.

So now you have the power to create what you want now more than ever ~ with this book.

Use your power wisely.

Blessings on your journey of Universal Love, Peace, LIGHT, Balance & Harmony.

HAPPY MANIFESTING!!!!

May the everlasting embers
of the stars be your guide
to remember all that you
truly are.…

We are all made of
stardust and a whole lot of
love.

Hatred isn't birthed. It is
Created.
&
Only Love can heal that.

Jessica Hope William's

Author of "Manifestation Mantras
for Soul Healing,
Self Mastery, & Creating a
Better Life."

About the Author:

Jessica grew up very poor and had incurred many traumas throughout her life, including abuse, sexual assault & severe domestic violence. Through this she had to spend many years learning to heal these traumas through many different healing modalities. It is through this gift of pain she was given that she learned to take her power back and create something beautiful. Thus her healing teachings & practice was born.

Jessica has been an Energy Healing Master & Teacher for over 10 years, specializing in ancient healing techniques, practices, divine channeling, soul healing & activation. She has used her mantras to assist in the healing of many clients over the years & she understands the power of the mind being interconnected to the energy field of the person; combining both together to master the manifestation abilities of the person using this technique.

Jessica has witnessed deep inner healing and transformation using these practices as well as her own healing practices in many people over the years and her hope is to inspire a deeper; Heart, Mind, Body, Soul Healing in all who use her practices.

Among several forms of therapy Jessica has been trained in, she is a Master & Teacher of Reiki Energy Healing, Angelic Healing, hamanic Healing - She is a Rite holder of the Munay Ki Shaman Lineage.

Jessica is also a Quantum Healing Hypnotherapist and Past Life Regression Therapist. Additionally she does Intimacy and Tantric Coaching and Workshops. DNA Healing & Activation work is Unique to her innate Gifts and Abilities.

Jessica is also a Divine Soul Reader and Spiritual Guide for those seeking guidance and answers on a soul level and has been for over 15 years. Her clients are the proof of her work.

Jessica's passion is helping people find the power within themselves to live a brighter & higher quality of life. To heal on all levels. To live with purpose & Intention.

As a Master of Usui, Tibetan,
Arc Angelic & Ascended
Master Healing.
I Practice multiple forms of
Powerful Healing and Energy
Soul and Spirit Work.
I am a shaman of the
Munay Ki Lineage.
I am a Quantum Healing
Hypnotherapist &
Tantric Intimacy Coach,
Divine Soul Channel / Reader / Guide.

I Am now bringing forth
My own form of divine healing
work: DNA Activation
& Ascension Activation Healing.

Jessica Hope Williams

Message to the reader:

May the universe within you and all
around you guide you to the answers and
the healing that you deserve.

May you learn to love your life and see its
beauty even in the imperfections –
All life is sacred & beautiful.

May we transcend the hatred on this planet into love,
universal peace & ultimately into mutual
respect between our sisters & our
brothers on earth.
As above – So below.
Remember ~ We Are Sacred.

Jessica Hope William's

Author of "Manifestation Mantras
for Soul Healing,
Self Mastery, & Creating a
Better Life."